anniversary.

May your days together be full
of laughter, new delights, and a
shared contentment.

May you always be yourselves
– yet one – in love and kindness
and in understanding.

To: *Betty and Bill*

From: *Norman and
Judith
with love*

You were born together,
and together you shall be
for evermore.
You shall be together when
the white wings of death
scatter your days.
Aye, you shall be together
even in the silent memory
of God.
But let there be spaces in
your togetherness.
And let the winds of the
heavens dance between you.

KAHLIL GIBRAN (1883-1931),
from *The Prophet*

To love someone means to be involved with, to identify with, to engage with, to suffer with and for them, and to share their joys.

WILLARD GAYLIN, b. 1925

In a successful marriage, there is no such thing as one's way. There is only the way of both, only the bumpy, dusty, difficult, but always mutual path!

PHYLLIS MCGINLEY

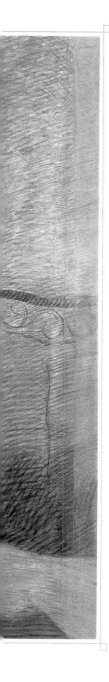

The supreme happiness of
life is the conviction that we
are loved; loved for
ourselves, or rather, loved
in spite of ourselves.

VICTOR HUGO (1802-1885)

A good partnership is passion and
monotony, practicalities, magic,
talk and tears and laughter. And
at the core lies a secret place,
where strangers cannot enter. A
place of trust and love and deep
content. Its living heart.

PAM BROWN, b.1928

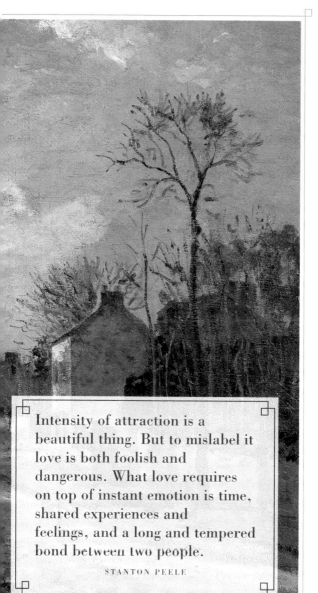

Intensity of attraction is a
beautiful thing. But to mislabel it
love is both foolish and
dangerous. What love requires
on top of instant emotion is time,
shared experiences and
feelings, and a long and tempered
bond between two people.

STANTON PEELE

At the end of what is called
the "sexual life" the only
love which has lasted is the
love which has everything,
every disappointment,
every failure and every
betrayal, which has
accepted even the sad fact
that in the end there is no
desire so deep as the simple
desire for companionship.

GRAHAM GREENE (1904-1991)

In the consciousness of
belonging together, in the
sense of constancy, resides
the sanctity, the beauty of
matrimony, which helps us
to endure pain more easily,
to enjoy happiness doubly,
and to give rise to the
fullest and finest
development of our nature.

FANNY LEWALD (1811–1889)

To be rooted is perhaps the most important and least recognized need of the human soul.

SIMONE WEIL (1909-1943),
from *The Need for Roots*

Knowing is the most profound kind of love, giving someone the gift of knowledge about yourself.

MARSHA NORMAN

Age does not protect you from love. But love, to some extent, protects you from age.

JEANNE MOREAU, b.1928

All love at first, like generous wine,
Ferments and frets, until 'tis fine;
But when 'tis settled on the lee,
And from the impurer matter free,
Becomes the richer still, the older,
And proves the pleasanter, the colder.

SAMUEL BUTLER (1835-1902)

Sing and dance together and be
joyous, but let each one of you be
alone,
Even as the strings of a lute are
alone though they quiver with the
same music.

KAHLIL GIBRAN (1883-1931),
from *The Prophet*

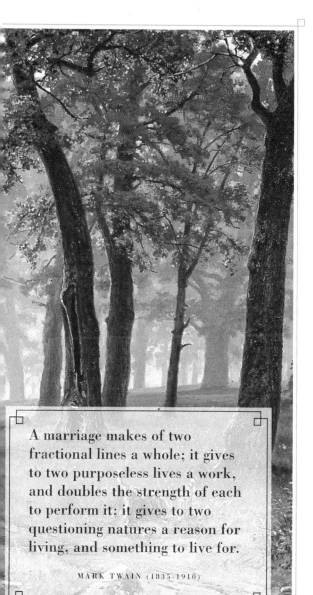

A marriage makes of two
fractional lines a whole; it gives
to two purposeless lives a work,
and doubles the strength of each
to perform it; it gives to two
questioning natures a reason for
living, and something to live for.

MARK TWAIN (1835-1910)